A Vanished World

WILFRED THESIGER

A Vanished World

HarperCollins*Publishers*

By the same author

ARABIAN SANDS

THE MARSH ARABS

DESERT, MARSH AND MOUNTAIN

VISIONS OF A NOMAD

THE LIFE OF MY CHOICE

MY KENYA DAYS

THE DANAKIL DIARY

AMONG THE MOUNTAINS

HarperCollins*Publishers*
77–85 Fulham Palace Road,
Hammersmith, London W6 8JB

www.fireandwater.com

Published by HarperCollins*Publishers* 2001
Produced in association with Motivate Publishing, Dubai
9 8 7 6 5 4 3 2 1

A catalogue record for this book
is available from the British Library

ISBN 0 00 7108370

Set in Quadraat

Production: Arjen Jansen

Printed and bound in Belgium by
Proost NV, Turnhout

FRONTISPIECE: Bal Qarn

To the memory of Mollie Emtage

ACKNOWLEDGEMENTS

Without the help of Alexander Maitland, my biographer and very close friend, this book could never have been written. I am also grateful for the help of Dr Elizabeth Edwards and Lynn Parker of the Pitt Rivers Museum; Mike Shaw and Jonathan Pegg at Curtis Brown; my editors Lucinda McNeile and Tamsin Miller; to Philip Lewis who helped to select the pictures and designed the layout and to Ian Fairservice of Motivate Publishing who conceived the book and worked with me on the picture selection.

I STARTED TO TAKE PHOTOGRAPHS when I hunted in the Danakil country immediately after I had attended Haile Selassie's coronation, but these early photographs are just 'snaps' – evocative for me but of no artistic merit. This is a pity, for I had the opportunity to get some magnificent photographs among the Danakil, and later in the Sudan and during the war in Ethiopia, but at the time I had little care for photography. I just pointed the camera and pressed the button. Only while I was in Arabia after the war did I begin to consider the composition of each photograph. . . anxious to achieve the best possible result.

From then on, as I travelled, I took photographs of magnificent mountain scenery, of sculptural sand dunes and of forests, of wild animals and architecture of many kinds. But by far the greatest number of photographs were of people, for it was they who afforded me the most interesting subjects. Some of them remained my companions over the years; some were with me for a month or two; others I met by chance in villages or at wells.

I used an old-fashioned Kodak belonging to my father during my Danakil journey and took many photos. I bought a Leica II before going to the Sudan in 1934 and used this camera until 1959, when I returned to Ethiopia. I possessed no additional lenses until I went to the Marshes in southern Iraq; then I bought an Elmarit/90 portrait lens and an Elmarit/35 wide-angle lens, but I still took most of my photographs with the standard lens. I changed my Leica II for a Leicaflex in 1959 and have used this camera ever since. When I went to Kenya I added an Elmarit/135 to my other lenses for photographing animals.

I have taken all my photographs through a yellow filter, to which I have sometimes added a polaroid filter at higher altitudes. I have never used a flash and in order to travel light have never carried a tripod. In Arabia I kept my camera in a goat-skin bag to protect it from the sand – and have done so ever since. I have always used Ilford films. A month or even a year often elapsed before I could get them developed. I kept each roll in an airtight container and only in Indonesia were some of my films affected by humidity.

★

Moussa Hamma, my *shikari* (left) and Muhammad Sirage, my *aban*.

One of the *janalis* at Bahdu.

I have never taken a colour photograph, nor have I ever felt the urge to do so. This may be due in part to my preference for drawings rather than paintings, my appreciation of line rather than colour. I am, however, convinced that black and white photography affords a wider and more interesting scope than colour, which by its very nature aims to reproduce exactly what is seen by the photographer. Nonetheless, until recently many of the colours were badly reproduced and the pictures suffered in consequence. Now, because of its accuracy, colour photography lends itself ideally to objects or scenes that are naturally brightly coloured – to animals, birds, or ceremonial occasions, for example.

With black and white film, on the other hand, each subject offers its own variety of possibilities, according to the use made by the photographer of light and shade. This is particularly the case with portraits, which are my chief interest. Indeed, I believe that the majority of the photographs in this book have a quality that would have been lost in colour.

The photographs which follow illustrate the challenges and rewards of my travelling and photography. I have been welcomed in remote, seldom-visited regions, such as the Hazarjat or Nuristan in Afghanistan, because I was accompanied by inhabitants of those areas. Accepted by them, I was able to take photographs of these striking people, who, knowing nothing about photography, adopted no self-conscious poses. This is not easy to achieve in more sophisticated areas. When I first went to northern Kenya I took many photographs of relaxed and graceful tribesmen. Now, with the influx of tourists, all anxious to get photos, they have learnt to pose and demand money. Some, however, resent this intrusion and I have heard them protest: 'We are not wild animals to be photographed. ' I have refrained from taking photographs, except from a distance, in places where I am not known and accepted. Some years ago, when I motored for a month in Rajasthan, I stayed each night in a local rest-house. I took many photographs of forts and temples, but no portraits of people.

As a photographer I have found that apart from getting the exposure and depth of field correct, other considerations have affected the success of a photograph. For example, the exact moment caught or lost for ever: a gap in clouds framing a mountain peak; a pattern of shadows on a desert landscape with a group of men and camels exactly placed; a street scene that depends on the position of a moving figure; a passing canoe reflected in the water; a leopard disturbed on its prey.

★

The scenery of the desert, the marshes, or the mountains which I photographed will endure, but the way of life of the tribesmen I was with has either changed completely, like that of the Bedu, or, as in Ethiopia, has been altered by events beyond their control.

I am glad I took so many portraits, for most of them can never be repeated. They fascinate me as I look at them, reminding me vividly of my many and varied companions and of many a chance encounter. They were taken under all sorts of conditions and in a variety of light, but it was photography very different from studio portraiture. I tried to catch the turn or lift of a head, the set of the mouth, the reflection in the eyes and the combination of highlights and shadow on the face, to get an effective picture. As with all photographs, the composition was important, the background and the set and texture of clothes. Most of my pictures are of men, for I lived most of the time in a man's world, often among Muslims.

Though I know little about the technique of photography and am lost when someone discusses the workings of a camera or the processing of a film, I have an instinctive sense of composition. I always try to frame a photograph so that there is no need to cut it, but this is often impossible.

Occasionally, and sometimes purely by chance, everything – exposure, focus and the composition – coincided to produce a photograph which still continues to satisfy me. Over the years I have enlarged and captioned the ones which I consider to be the best or most interesting.

When I browse among my seventy albums of these selected photographs, my most cherished possessions, I live once more in a vanished world.

WILFRED THESIGER
2001

WILFRED THESIGER, AGED TWENTY, began to take photographs with a Kodak roll-film box-camera, which his father had used in the Belgian Congo and brought with him to Abyssinia in 1909, the year before Thesiger was born.

Some of his earliest photographs were taken during a hunting trip in the Danakil country which followed Haile Selassie's coronation as Emperor of Abyssinia at Addis Ababa, in 1930. His photographs from the Danakil included groups of wild-looking tribesmen with their camels, and portraits of Moussa Hamma and Muhammad Sirage, his guides.

At first, Thesiger used a camera, like an extension of his hand-written diaries, to simply record people, places and things seen during his journeys. His photographs improved, both technically and artistically, when he travelled in Arabia after the Second World War. From then on, Thesiger noted, 'photography became a major interest'. The visual impact of the Arabian deserts, the emotional stimulus of danger, physical hardship, and companionships with certain Bedu tribesmen, notably, Salim bin Kabina and Salim bin Ghabaisha, inspired superb photographs including many of Thesiger's finest portraits.

From taking snapshots to producing photographic works of art certainly represents an enormous advance for any photographer. Although Thesiger has told us where and how this happened: 'Only while I was in Arabia did I begin to consider the composition of each photograph,' he has never attempted to explain *why*, from his point of view. As a literary equivalent, Thesiger's tour de force – transforming his Arabian diaries into the elegant, spare prose of *Arabian Sands* – involved yet another, to this day largely undocumented venture into the unknown. Writing *Arabian Sands* in Denmark and Ireland, he was guided by his literary agent and friends who read the manuscript in its early stages; whereas, the effort to produce better photographs was his alone.

Thesiger's increasing fascination with camera portraiture mirrored his already selective interest in remote peoples. Taking photographs of charismatic tribesmen appealed to him far more than merely recording a tribe's customs or

Members of my expedition; Umar is in the centre with Kassimi on his right.

rituals, as his portraits of a Danakil *janili*, or soothsayer, and an eighteen-year-old Asaimara chief, Hamdo Ouga, show. The *janili*, a man of considerable status, was renowned for his prophecies. The handsome young chief who had recently killed four Issa tribesmen seemed to Thesiger 'the Danakil equivalent of a nice, rather self-conscious Etonian who had just won his school colours for cricket'.

In the Danakil country, Thesiger had depended on his Somali headman, Umar, but was never 'on close terms' with him. Umar, dressed smartly in a turban, khaki shirt and shorts, stands at the centre of a group-portrait, rather like an end-of-term school photograph, which Thesiger dutifully took of his followers.

Sixty years later, Thesiger recalled: 'There was no feeling of friendship for Umar. A great respect, reliance, but he was in no sense my friend.' Umar 'had ensured the loyalty of my men, accurate information. . . and his imperturbability had given me the assurance that I had sometimes needed.'

Thesiger photographed his caravan, his encampments, Danakil tribesmen watering their camels at wells, grave-monuments, attractive valleys and extraordinary sights, such as Danakil swimming their sheep and goats across the Awash river. Most of his photographs (including those published in *The Danakil Diary*, 1996) were taken in 1934, during the second stage of his expedition, through Aussa, to the Awash river's end. Yet on this arduous, often dangerous, journey Thesiger found little time for photography. His daily tasks had included mapping, shooting birds or animals and preserving their skins, gathering as much information as he could about the Danakil, and recording in his notebooks, or with sketches, details of the landscape and geology of their country.

The ornithologist, David Haig-Thomas, Thesiger's companion during the preliminary stage of his Danakil expedition, advised him to buy the Leica II 35mm miniature camera which he took with him to the Sudan in December 1934. Thesiger recalled: 'The Leica gave me the right weapon. With this camera I had the means to take really good photographs.'

Although a hand-held light-meter was needed to ensure accurate exposures, the compact, solidly-build Leica II, with its distinctive coupled range-finder and superb lenses, was ideally suited for travel-photography. Thesiger commented: 'Using a manual camera, you had to work for the results. To me, this was the point of it.' The various cameras in the Leica II range had been designed to accommodate screw-attached Elmar or Summar lenses. Later, instead of replacing the faithful Leica II, Thesiger had his camera fitted with an adaptor to enable him to use bayonet-pattern Elmarit lenses introduced after the Second World War.

He had an 'instinctive sense of composition', but admitted to possessing little technical knowledge of photography. An old friend and admirer, the late Ronald Codrai, himself an excellent photographer, regarded Thesiger as 'a very great picture-taker', but someone who was never really interested in photography, as such. Before he arrived in the Sudan, Thesiger had been deeply influenced by the French pearl-fisherman, Henri de Monfried's *Aventures de Mer* and *Les Secrets de la Mer Rouge*. He had bought de Monfried's books in 1933 at Addis Ababa, and read them at intervals throughout his Danakil journey. Crossing by dhow from Tajura to Jibuti some months later (true to de Monfried's spirit) he shared the crew's evening meal of rice and fish.

Thesiger said:

Travelling with my party, among the Danakil, I lived as a white man. There was never any feeling of getting on terms with the men who were with me, or with the people we encountered. It would have been inconceivable that I'd gone over and sat with my men at their fire. Umar would have been astounded had I done this. On that first journey I lived and travelled very much as my father would have travelled. But when we sailed in the dhow from Tajura, I sat there on deck and ate supper with the crew, and I realized that this was what I wanted to do from then on.

Soon after Thesiger arrived in northern Darfur, a young Zaghawi tribesman, Idris Daud, became his personal retainer and constant companion. Idris was the first of many tribal companions with whom he established a close relationship, and Thesiger's photographs revealed unmistakable evidence of this bond. A typical example, illustrated in Thesiger's autobiography, *The Life of My Choice* (1987), shows Idris and five other Zaghawa beside a dead lioness. On this occasion, catching 'the lift of [Idris's] head, the set of [his] mouth', was more important to Thesiger than merely photographing the dangerous animal he had tracked and killed.

In another photograph Wilfred stands near Idris in the dappled shadow of some trees. This unpublished snapshot marks a watershed between Thesiger, the self-conscious European, distanced from his tribal followers, and Thesiger, their companion, determined to live with them on equal terms. The slightly blurred image of Thesiger and Idris suggests a very precise metaphor for this gradual transition, as the way of life Thesiger desired most began gradually to merge with the life he actually led.

Pre-war compositions, such as 'A gathering of the Maidob in northern Dafur' and another of Thesiger's Nuer porters wading thigh-deep across a flooded plain, had been distanced, impersonal, but more accomplished than many of his previous photographs. 'My trophies', a set-piece dated 1938, shows Idris and Thesiger's interpreter, Malo, aboard the Sudan Political Service's paddle steamer, *Kereri* – Thesiger's district headquarters – on either side of a symmetrical display of preserved skins, horns, skulls and tusks. The contrived perspective emphasized by the *Kereri*'s tall funnel, the arched roof of the wheel-house, the taff-rails sharply converging, confirms Thesiger's eye for a dramatic setting. In other versions of the composition, photographed by Idris or by Malo with a pre-set Leica II, Thesiger has substituted himself for Malo or Idris.

The statuesque, naked Nuer appealed to his taste for linear and sculptural forms. Published in *The Life of My Choice*, a group-photograph titled 'My porters' captures seven Nuer in slightly different attitudes, facing mainly away from the camera. Here, Thesiger's instinctive response to his subject, and 'the magic moment', have coincided to produce an extremely successful photograph. An emphatic gesture made by one of the Nuer is repeated, quite by chance, by others in the group. The men's actions unify Thesiger's composition, just as their varied poses bring to life an otherwise uneventful scene.

Thesiger has an aesthetic preference for shades of dark, rather than white skin-colour. In his own words: 'It was a cultural thing. I simply wasn't interested

Asaimara warriors at Bahdu wearing killing decorations. Hamdo Ouga is on the left. The thongs hanging from their daggers indicate how many men each of them had killed. Hamdo Ouga himself was killed a few days later.

in photographing Europeans. I wanted to record the people I was with, and those I encountered, in other countries like Abyssinia and Arabia.'

During the Second World War, Thesiger might easily have photographed such army officers as Orde Wingate, Gerald de Gaury and David Stirling with whom he served in Ethiopia, Syria and North Africa. To his lasting regret he never did so.

Instead, in Syria, Thesiger photographed the Druzes, among them his orderly Faris Shahin, and Faris's white-bearded grandfather. Other wartime portraits – one of a Druze cavalryman, another showing Druze elders grouped among Roman ruins – were formal, purposeful, yet still impersonal; utterly different in approach and character to the intimate portraits Thesiger would take, years later, in Arabia. Until after the war, photography had remained a pastime to which Thesiger still attached no great importance. Only then did he begin to photograph subjects at close quarters, avoiding unnecessary background, concentrating on expressive details such as eyes, mouth or the texture of their clothing.

Thesiger's interest in portraiture may have been aroused by Bertram Thomas's photographs of Bedu in *Arabia Felix* (1932), which, though informative, did not seem (to Thesiger) to say anything. Or (more probably), by Freya Stark's close-ups of tribesmen illustrating *Seen in the Hadhramaut* (1939). Yet, Thesiger insists:

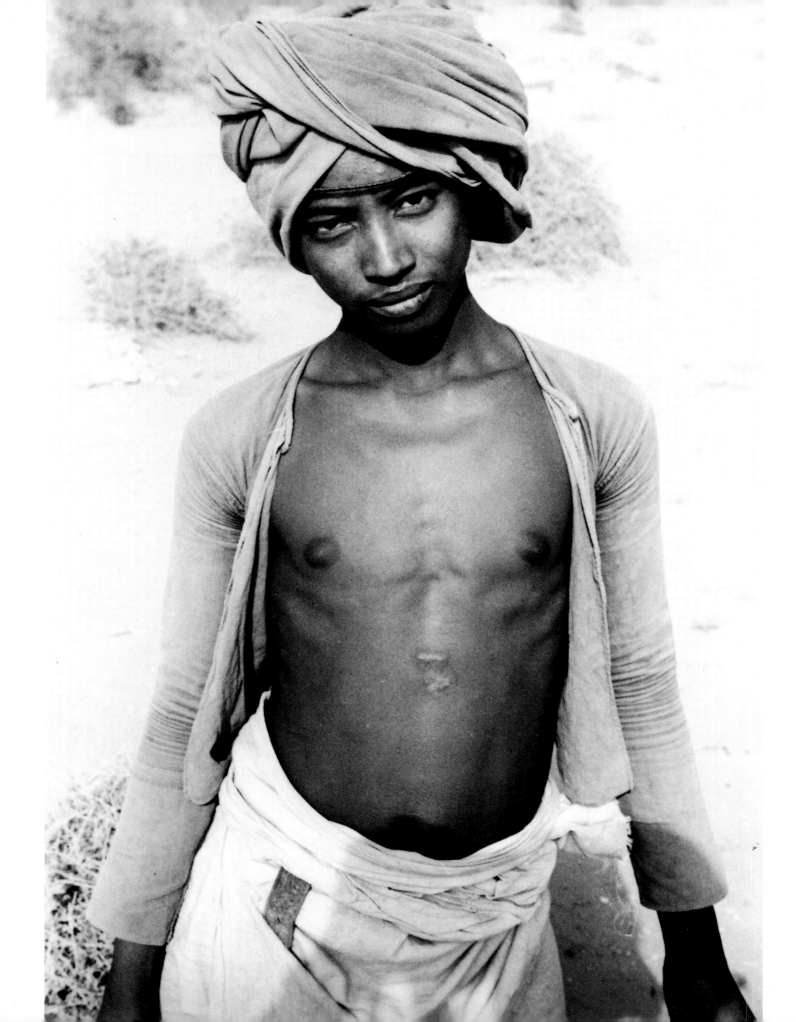

'I didn't really think in this way, making these connections. It just happened. I do remember looking at Freya Stark's book. . . As I went on taking more photographs, they gradually improved. I'd think, there's a good subject; and I would sense immediately how to compose it.' Whatever influenced Thesiger at this period, his already obvious gifts for composition and portraiture would be given full reign in the deserts of Arabia, where he mainly lived and travelled between 1945 and 1950.

Today Thesiger's name is inseparable from Arabia and the Bedu. There is no doubt that many of his finest photographs were taken in Arabia, including the magnificent portraits and desert landscapes associated with his two crossings of the Empty Quarter, in 1946–47 and 1947–48. While Thesiger does not dispute this, he firmly believes that a great many photographs he took years later in Iraq, the Hindu Kush, the Karakorams, Kenya, India and Ladakh, are just as successful in terms of their negative quality, content and composition.

Over the years, Thesiger acquired several fine drawings and engravings by the eighteenth-century Venetian artist, Tiepolo; and an atmospheric Mediter-ranean landscape drawn by Edward Lear. The Arabian desert's evocation of space, line and form could not fail to appeal to anyone who, like Thesiger, preferred drawings and classical sculpture to paintings. As an expression of idealized male physique, Thesiger considered Donatello's slender *David* far superior to the heavily-muscled *David* sculpted by Michelangelo. Thesiger's appreciation of Donatello's *David* equated very precisely to his admiration for the Nuer of southern Sudan: tribesmen, he wrote, 'with graceful figures of track athletes. In general they had fine features, and I thought what superb models they would make for a sculptor.'

In February 1939, at Toldoi in Kordofan, Thesiger first saw the 'naked and pagan' Nuba, 'more massively built than the Nuer, as became a race whose sport was wrestling'. The savage power evoked by Thesiger's photographs of Nuba wrestlers counterpointed studies of Nuer herdsmen and others of his porters on trek or in repose. The Nuba's powerful physique contrasted with the athletic build of the Nuer, just as each, in turn, mirrored a *David* interpreted by Michelangelo or Donatello.

The nomadic Bedu, with whom Thesiger travelled in Arabia after the Second World War, proved to be tremendously hardy, fit and capable of great endurance. Although they were much smaller than the Nuer, many of whom towered above Thesiger's six feet two inches, the Bedu were no less graceful or poised. Among them Thesiger found excellent subjects for portraiture, including two young Rashid, Salim bin Kabina and Salim bin Ghabaisha, who travelled with him in the Empty Quarter and became closely attached to him.

A now-familiar photograph, taken in 1946, of bin Ghabaisha – alert, brooding, defiant, like a resting bird of prey – embodies Thesiger's attraction to nomadic, desert Arab tribes and the Arabian desert and everything connected with it. By comparison, his photograph of bin Kabina, in a desert setting, both romanticizes and isolates the young Bedu whose sombre profile and long, tangled hair give him an almost Messianic pathos. A recurrent theme in Thesiger's portraiture has been the 'isolated figure totally encompassed by wilderness'; or, like bin Kabina, captured in a remote, almost surreal landscape stripped of natural features – an effective visual metaphor for Thesiger's concept of the 'unknown'. At other times, Thesiger disengages his subjects completely from their surroundings, photographing them (sometimes posed on rocks) from a low angle, with the sky a neutral background. In this context, Thesiger's preference for black and white photography is especially significant. According to Elizabeth Edwards, curator of the Pitt Rivers Museum, 'it is, by its very nature, an essentialist medium, expressing line, tone and texture rather than the distractions of colour with its stronger insistence on an analogical realism'.

No less dramatic are photographs of Thesiger's companions made insignificant by the desert's vast landscape, to which they give a sense of human scale: bin Kabina in the shadow of a dune; men and camels descending from a ridge; somewhere in the Empty Quarter, a string of camels led by a single, armed Bedu.

Again and again, such potent images of the desert's 'primordial solitude' reinforce the bond between Thesiger and his companions, reminding us that 'distance is not the measure of remoteness'. No longer content merely to record people, places and events, Thesiger gives artistic permanence to man's faint imprint upon the wilderness. With consummate skill, he interprets the scenic image and, at the same time, hallmarks the image seen.

Thesiger's Arabian journeys provided a continuous motif for photography; a motif repeated already throughout his pre-war photography in Abyssinia, Sudan and the French Sahara. A sense of interrupted movement charges with tension Thesiger's photographs of his party resting beside their camels. His finest prose reflects the aesthetic and romantic appeal of his desert photography, documenting with poignant precision the hardships and intangible rewards of the Bedu's nomadic world. 'There,' Thesiger writes, 'distances were measured in hours on camel-back, and over all lay a silence that we have now driven from our world. In the Empty Quarter we endured almost incessant hunger and, worse still, thirst, sometimes for days on end rationing ourselves to a pint [of water] a day; there was the heat of a blazing sun in a shadeless land; the bitter cold of winter nights; incessant watchfulness for raiders, our rifles always at hand; anxiety that our camels, on which our lives depended, would collapse.'

In *The Life of My Choice* he acknowledged:

It is difficult to analyse the motive that induced me to make those journeys, or the satisfaction I derived from such a life. There was of course the lure of the unknown; there was the constant test of resolution and endurance. Yet, those travels in the Empty Quarter would have been for me a pointless penance but for the comradeship of my Bedu companions. . . they possessed a freedom which we, with all our craving for possessions, cannot experience. . . I have never forgotten their open-handed generosity. . . their total honesty; their pride in themselves and in their tribe; their loyalty to each other and not least to me, a stranger of alien faith from an unknown land.

The intensity of this experience set Thesiger's imagination afire, resulting in photographs of unprecedented power and beauty. A decade later, his imperishable memories of five years with the Bedu inspired Thesiger to write his first book, *Arabian Sands* (1959), which is now widely acknowledged as his masterpiece.

In 1950, when political circumstances beyond his control barred Thesiger from further contact with the Bedu, his search for 'an alternative to the desert' led him first to Kurdistan, and later to the Marshes of southern Iraq. From then until 1958, he divided his time mainly between the Marshes and the 'stupendous mountains' of Asia – the Hindu Kush and the Karakorams.

In *The Marsh Arabs*, published in 1964, Thesiger described the appeal which this remote area held for him: 'Memories of that first visit to the Marshes have never left me: firelight on a half-turned face, the crying of geese, duck flying in to feed, a boy's voice singing somewhere in the dark. . .' Whereas in Arabia he had lived for months at a time with a small, closely-knit group, in the Marshes he fed and slept in villages, sharing to the full the communal life of the Madan, or Marsh Arabs. Thesiger's Iraqi portraits and landscapes mirror his changed surroundings where, apart from travels about the Marshes by canoe, the journey as a motif is absent.

Captivated by the Madan and their world, Thesiger portrayed a new generation of tribal companions, including his canoemen, Amara, Sabaiti, Hasan and Yasin. Besides boat-builders, dancers, fishermen and weavers, Thesiger photographed tribesmen hunting wild boar, house-building, harvesting reeds for fodder and herding the black buffaloes round which villagers' lives revolved.

Once again, among the Marsh Arabs, he was able to establish close comradeships and communicate easily with the people he encountered. Accepted by the Madan, he was able to take as many photographs as he wished. In doing so, Thesiger recorded countless, beautiful images of a centuries-old culture and a way of life which, four decades later, would be destroyed for ever.

By contrast, among the mountains of western Asia, where Thesiger travelled for months each year to escape the unbearably humid, hot Marsh summers, intimate contact with the people was denied him. In Pakistan and Afghanistan, he had to rely almost entirely on local, English-speaking interpreters; unlike Nasser Hussain, Thesiger's Arabic-Kurdish interpreter in Iraqi Kurdistan, they were never included among his published photographs of Asia's mountain tribes.

Thesiger commented:

On these journeys among the mountains of Kurdistan, Pakistan and Afghanistan, I had passed through some of the most spectacular country in the world and I had encountered people of many different races and origins, from Mongols to Nuristanis and Pathans. They varied greatly in their customs, the clothes they wore and in the lives they led; but all were Muslims, and this gave me a basic understanding of their behaviour. Though I had managed, in Peshawar and Kabul, to find someone who spoke English and was willing to accompany me, my inability to speak any of their languages kept me apart from my porters on these journeys and deprived me of the sense of comradeship I had known in Arabia and among the Madan in Iraq.

Despite this handicap, Thesiger took many fine portraits of Tajiks, Kafirs, Kirghiz, Turis, Hazaras, Nuristanis, Pashaies, Kandaris and Kuchis. As always, he respected the customs and ethics of these remote peoples. In the Hindu Kush, after his now-famous encounter with Eric Newby and Hugh Carless, near the Chamar Pass, Thesiger noted: 'Not far from here we stopped at another *ailoq* [a summer pasture camp] with only women and girls in it. None of them would come near us. . . When we had met at Shanaize, Newby told me that he had had a lot of difficulty photographing the girls; this was inevitable since all these people were Muslims.'

In 1959, the camera manufacturer, Leitz, invited Thesiger to test an

OPPOSITE Tribesman at a Hajar village near Meshed.

un-numbered prototype of their Leicaflex single-lens reflex camera. Thesiger used this Leicaflex in Ethiopia and, in due course, replaced it with a numbered 'trade' version of his own. Although he had found the semi-automatic Leicaflex more convenient than his Leica II, he never for a moment regretted having used a manual camera. In 1997 Thesiger advised a friend: 'Start with a manual. You do the work yourself. The automatic camera gives you what it can do.'

Travelling south through Ethiopia, in 1959, the first of Thesiger's journeys with the Leicaflex ended at Mega, near the Kenya border. At Moyale, on the Kenya side of the border, the District Commissioner, George Webb, gave him detailed information about the Boran, Somalis and northern Kenya tribes. These included the Turkana and the pastoral Samburu, among whom Thesiger was destined to live for more than twenty years.

In November 1960, Webb helped Thesiger obtain permission to travel in a restricted area of Kenya, then known as the Northern Frontier District. Thesiger found magnificent opportunities for portraiture among the nomadic and pastoral tribes – the Rendille, 'the Boran, the Turkana, who were as naked as the Nuer, and the Samburu, an offshoot of the famous Masai'.

With his new camera, in northern Tanganyika (now Tanzania), he photographed the proud Masai, whose lifestyle 'remained largely unchanged from the days when the earliest explorers met them.' Since his youth. Thesiger had sought 'savagery and colour'. He admired the Masai, 'handsome arrogant warriors, with their red-pigmented hair and red cloth draped negligently over a shoulder [who] still carried long-bladed spears and distinctive heraldic shields, and guarded great herds of cattle.'

After an interlude of five years, Thesiger returned to Kenya in 1968. He continued to travel in the Northern Frontier District until 1976; from then until 1994, much of his time was spent at Maralal, a small township eighty miles north of the equator, where he lived in a succession of houses he had built for his Samburu companions, Lawi Leboyare and Laputa Lekakwar, and their families.

Apart from the photographs he took in Kenya, during those years, some of his best portraits were taken in Ladakh, which he visited, aged seventy-three, in 1983, travelling from village to village with Sir Robert ffolkes on ponies or yaks.

At Maralal, Thesiger resented the intrusion into tribal life of casual visitors who imposed themselves and their cameras on passers-by or at Samburu initiation ceremonies, which he had been able to photograph extensively due to his close relationship with members of the tribe. Thesiger remembered how, years earlier, the Masai in Tanzania had refused his first attempts to photograph them: 'I went off and started focusing my camera at various objects in the distance. After a while, one or two Masai came over and asked me what I was doing. I said, "Why don't you look through the camera?" which they did. After that, they became enthusiastic and I was able to take as many photographs of them as I wanted.'

Now in his ninetieth year, Wilfred Thesiger is as highly acclaimed for photography as for his writing. Without exception, all the books he has produced since 1959 have been illustrated – sometimes lavishly – by him; indeed, *Visions of a Nomad*, published in 1987, is devoted almost entirely to photographs.

Since October 1993, Thesiger's photographic collection, including 25,000 negatives and thousands of high-quality prints, has been housed at the Pitt Rivers Museum, Oxford. According to Elizabeth Edwards, the Museum's Curator of Photographs: 'Although [Thesiger's] subject matter encompasses the "ethnographic" the architectural and at times straight reportage, it is landscape and portraiture which dominate his photographic corpus. The photographs range from snapshot . . . to the consciously aesthetic. . . the informal to the formalist. . . In many ways the description "travel photography" is inadequate, for it suggests the transitory, culturally distanced and superficial. Thesiger's travels, writing and photography are none of these, being rather the product of a long-term committed and informed association with a region and its people. . . At another level these photographs record traditional ways of life in a world which has now changed beyond recognition, fractured by the gradual encroachment of "global culture", by development and political intervention. . . Consequently Thesiger's photographs are an invaluable historical source and it is as such that their "final home" is to be the archives of the Pitt Rivers Museum.'

In recent years Thesiger's photographs, his most treasured possessions, have compensated for his inability to read, due to failing sight. For this reason, like his vivid memories of past journeys, they have become increasingly important to him. 'Looking at my photographs today,' Thesiger concludes, 'I realize how much they have mattered to me over the years by keeping these impressions alive.'

ALEXANDER MAITLAND
London 2001

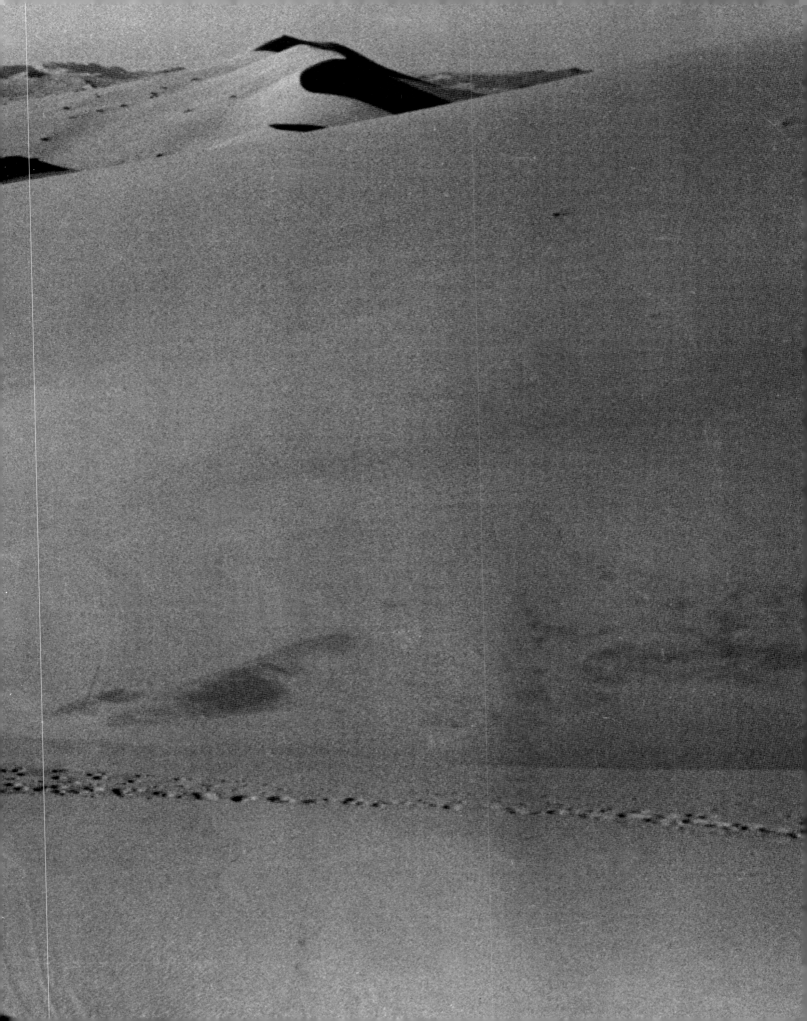

PREVIOUS PAGE The Empty Quarter, the sand desert within the great southern desert of Arabia, an area of almost half a million square miles, stretching from the Yemen border to Oman and from the southern coast of Arabia to the Arabian gulf.

BELOW Crossing the Empty Quarter.

OPPOSITE The Empty Quarter: Bedu and camels descending from a dune: some of the larger dunes were 500–700 feet high.

BELOW Arabia, a boy of the Sa'ar tribe.

OPPOSITE A tribesman of the Sa'ar, 'a pleasant, virile people who have been aptly described as "the wolves of the desert"'.

RIGHT Salim bin Ghabaisha, one of the Rashid and the author's guide, 1948.

BELOW One of the Sa'ar, northern Hadhramaut.

Salim bin Kabina, one of the author's Bedu guides.

ABOVE Boys of the Mahra tribe. The author passed through the Mahra country on his journey from Salala to Mukalla in 1947.

OPPOSITE A Mahra boy at Raidat al Mahra.

Camels resting at a well.

Sa'ar drawing water from a well. 'I noticed that they mixed rock-salt in it before watering their camels.'

A beautiful girl drawing water from a well at Manwakh. Her hair was braided, she wore silver ornaments and several necklaces – some of large cornelians, others of small white beads – and round her waist she had half a dozen silver chains.

Second from left Sheikh Zayid bin Sultan Al Nahyan, a highly respected leader of the Bedu, now the president of the United Arab Emirates.

At Buraimi, 1947, a hundred miles and four days' camel ride from Abu Dhabi,
in what is now the United Arab Emirates.

A brief halt to adjust a camel's load.

A Sa'ar family party on the move.

ABOVE A cheerful young tribesman of the Wahiba in Oman.

OPPOSITE The clean space of desert.

OVERLEAF The author's party.

PREVIOUS PAGE Saiwun, the largest town in the Hadhramaut, 1948.

OPPOSITE Shibam, Hadhramaut, a walled town with tall, closely-packed houses flanking silent alleyways.

BELOW Salim bin Ghabaisha.

The crew eating a meal aboard a dhow.

ABOVE On a dhow journey from Sharja to Bahrain.

OVERLEAF Sailors aboard an ocean-going *boom*, setting the mainsail
(Dubai-Bahrain).

FOLLOWING PAGE On Mount Hendron, a great 'rock-fist bastion' in
Iraqi Kurdistan, 1949.

Mount Hendron, 1949.

Musallim bin Al Kamam, the most widely travelled of the Rashid, one of the tribes in
southern Arabia which had adapted to life in the Empty Quarter.

ABOVE Muhammad bin Kalut of the Rashid tribe, 1948.

OPPOSITE One of the Sa'ar.

OVERLEAF A young saluki which the author had borrowed from Sheikh Zayid.

60   Mansoon man, 1949.

An elderly tribesman.

ABOVE On Mount Hendron.

LEFT The long range of Jabal al Akhadar (on the extreme right, behind Jabal Kaur), the Green Mountain which lies behind Muscat.

OVERLEAF Mountainous landscape near Mount Hendron, 1948.

FOLLOWING PAGE The author's party riding north across a gravel plain from Ibri to Muwaiqih beside the Oman mountains, accompanied by Sheikh Zayid's Bedu retainers, April 1949.

Northern Kurdistan 1950. A young Kurd of the Herki tribe in wide trousers made of strips of cloth, his jacket tucked into his cummerbund.

Northern Kurdistan 1950. Another young Kurd of the Herki tribe wearing striped clothes of a different pattern.

ABOVE Al Jabari of the Awamir tribe.

LEFT Crossing the Muqta to Abu Dhabi island.

ABOVE Sheikh Ali bin Said bin Rashid of the Yahahif at Habus, Wadi Andam, Oman.

OPPOSITE Huaishil, a sheikh of the Duru.

The author's party, Jabal al Akhadar.

A Mungur camp in Iraqi Kurdistan.

ABOVE Pizdhar (Kurdish) tribesmen.

OPPOSITE A watchtower, Jazirat al Hamra, Ras al Khaimah.

ABOVE A falconer with a hooded peregrine falcon which he was training and took
with him everywhere. The peregrine falcon is known to the Arabs as *shahin*.

OPPOSITE A coffee-maker.

ABOVE Huaishil

OPPOSITE The son of Huaishil, a Duru sheikh.

Boys of the Duru tribe, Oman.

ABOVE A Mungur boy on the Qandil range along the Iran-Iraq frontier. Like many Kurdish tribes, the Mungur move up to the mountains in spring with their cattle, sheep and goats, returning to their villages in autumn.

OPPOSITE A Pizdhar tribesman wearing his bandolier and fringed head dress. The Pizdhar are one of the Kurdish tribes.

A sheikh of the Barzan tribe in typical head dress and striped clothing.
'Of all the Kurdish tribes I liked the Barzan best.'

One of the Barzan.

Kurdish horsemen of the Pizdhar tribe.

OVERLEAF Among the Kurds.

ABOVE One of the Duru.

OPPOSITE In the Kurdish foothills, northeast of Mosul, northern Iraq.
Yazidi boys near the shrine of Sheikh Adi, founder of their community.

ABOVE A Yazidi in Jabal Sinjar

OPPOSITE Jews at Hajar

OVERLEAF Bal Qarn

BELOW Yazidis at a marriage and circumcision ceremony. 'There was much dancing and singing, in which the women joined.' Of Kurdish stock, the Yazidis live in villages west and northeast of Mosul.

OPPOSITE Sheikh Khalat of the Yazidis at Jabal Sinjar, a mountain in the desert west of Mosul. Sheikh Khalat's dress shows much influence of a style common among Sinjar Yazidis, many of whom wear Arab clothes.

ABOVE Part of the crowd which had gathered to watch a circumcision ceremony at sunset in the Tihama.

OPPOSITE Tihama, circumcision ceremony. The two boys to be circumcised are in front.

ABOVE Warid bin Shinta's eldest daughter.

OPPOSITE A tribesman.

ABOVE A Mahsud (scarred by smallpox) in southern Waziristan.

OPPOSITE A Mahsud near Wana, northwest frontier province.

OVERLEAF A festival in the Marshes of southern Iraq, 1953.

A Madan family mending rush mats.

Cultivators on the edge of the Marshes building a house, known as a *raba*, with
an entrance at either end. They are using giant reeds or *qasab* (*phragmites
communis*), a type of reed that grows to a height of twenty-five feet.

Marsh Arabs, 1952

The Iraqi Marshes: women washing copper bowls and cooking-pots.

In the Iraqi Marshes.

Madan boy at the prow of a *tarada*.

The Iraqi Marshes: Madan bringing fodder for their buffaloes.

Becalmed in the Marshes.

The Iraqi Marshes: a *sarifa*, a building of reeds and mats which has the roof supported by a ridge pole.

Madan spearing fish in the Marshes of southern Iraq. 'Each canoe had two occupants; one paddled, while the other stood in the bow and jabbed increasingly in the weeds.'

OVERLEAF The Iraqi Marshes: 'an isolated and beautiful world'.

The Iraqi Marshes: mats for export among the Bani Assad.

The Iraqi Marshes: mats and canoes.

ABOVE Ghilzai Kuchis in the Hazarajat, Afghanistan, 1954.

OPPOSITE The Hazarajat, Afghanistan, 1954. This boy has less-pronounced Mongolian features than many Hazaras.

OVERLEAF Al Essa celebrating the end of Ramadan, southern Iraq, 1955.

Boy with a mule, Morocco, 1955.

Morocco 1955

Morocco, 1955.

Morocco: a grain market, 1955.

Morocco: a market scene. 'I visited Morocco for the first time in 1937, when I went back there in 1955, I was escorted from one magnificent kasbah to another through the High Atlas.'

A Tigrean pilgrim in northern Ethiopia.

On the shore of Lake Tana, Ethiopia: 'The people here were the Waito . . . men and boys wore only a thick shamma, flung round to leave a shoulder bare.'

Ethiopia: a Fitaurari, or commander of the spearhead, with his wife.

ABOVE Southern Ethiopia, 1959: Boran with their camels.

OPPOSITE Pilgrims near Lalibela, northern Ethiopia. The man holds a crucifix.

ABOVE Iran: two of the Bakhtiari.

OPPOSITE Iran, 1964: a young Bakhtiari.

A Bakhtiari encampment, Iran.

With the Bakhtiari nomads, Iran.

ABOVE A Nuristani wearing a typical cap and embroidered waistcoat, 1965.

OPPOSITE The Nuristanis were 'born mountaineers' . . . 'with a streak of unpredictable violence in their nature.'

Kandari nomads coming down from Lake Shiva, above the Oxus valley, August 1965. 'I had seen the great tribes of northern Arabia – the Bakhtiari of Persia, the Herki of Kurdistan, and the Powindah coming down to Pakistan – yet for some reason, perhaps the landscape, my memory of the Kandaris remains the most vivid of them all.'

PREVIOUS PAGE Yemen, during the civil war: 'We came to a town where seven-storeyed houses were built of mud amd resembled the kasbahs of the High Atlas; but the centre of the town had been bombed to ruins.'

ABOVE Yemen – Tihama.

Yemen 1966: tribesman seated among buildings destroyed by fighting during the civil war.

ABOVE Yemen – an elderly Tihama.

OPPOSITE One of the Tihama, Yemen.

Boys at Qalat Razih in northern Yemen.

Women and children from the village of Artal hiding in nearby
caves after bombing following a Republican attack.

OPPOSITE Yemen, civil war: an Udhr tribesman, with houses and cultivated terraces in the background.

BELOW Royalist troops at the pass at Nagil Yasla, Yemen, 1967. The author visited Nagil Yasla two days after a battle in which Prince Hasan Ismail's force had thrown back the Republicans' artillery.

OVERLEAF Yemen, 1966: Tihama tribesmen, many wearing their distinctive large straw hats or plaited conical caps.

ABOVE A young Tihama.

OPPOSITE Yemen – Tihama boy.

ABOVE Yemen, 1966: Tihama soldiers; during the civil war I saw boys of this age fighting for the Royalist army.

OPPOSITE Tribesmen at Suq al Thuluth, Yemen.

OVERLEAF Yemen, 1966, an armed party on the move, during the civil war.

Boy at Suq al Thuluth in the Yemen.

Yemen – an Udhr boy.

At Suq al Badr in the Yemen, an uncircumcised boy of the Ghamar tribe.

A boy of the Ghamar tribe, Yemen.

PREVIOUS PAGE Samburu, new *moran* or warriors. The boy on the extreme right has the circular tuft of hair on his head, worn like this before circumcision takes place.

OPPOSITE Northern Kenya, circumcised Samburu boy with birds he has shot hanging down the nape of his neck.

BELOW The author's Samburu companion, Lawi Leboyare, 1977.

ABOVE Samburu youths in black goatskin capes. These capes, worn by initiates before circumcision, are made from three skins dyed with charcoal mixed with animal fat.

OPPOSITE Samburu: one of the *moran*.

Samburu mother shaving her son's head on the eve of his circumcision.

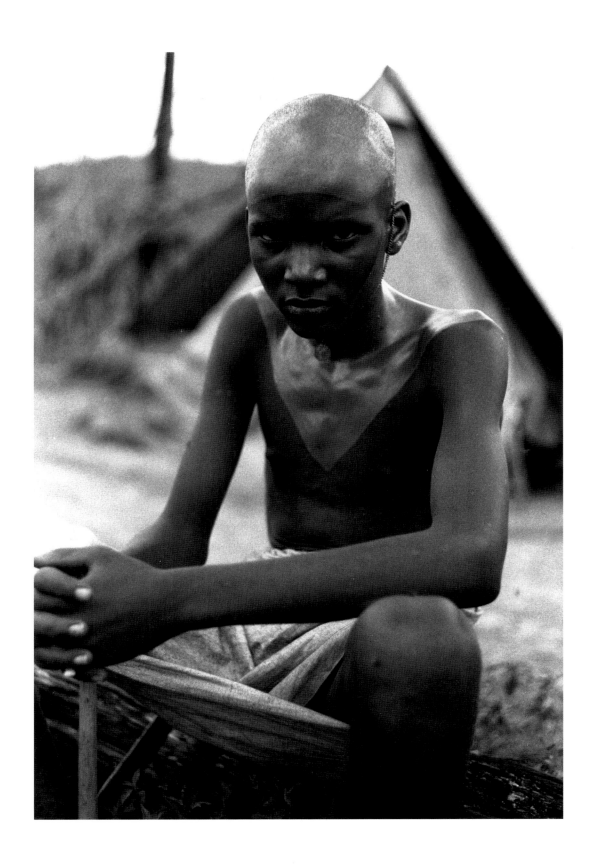

Lawi at the time of circumcision.

ABOVE A young Samburu wearing a goatskin cape.

OPPOSITE A Samburu elder, northern Kenya.

Samburu initiates chanting a *lebarta* (circumcision song).

Samburu: new *moran* chanting and dancing.

ABOVE Lawi

OPPOSITE Samburu coating an arrow point with gum.

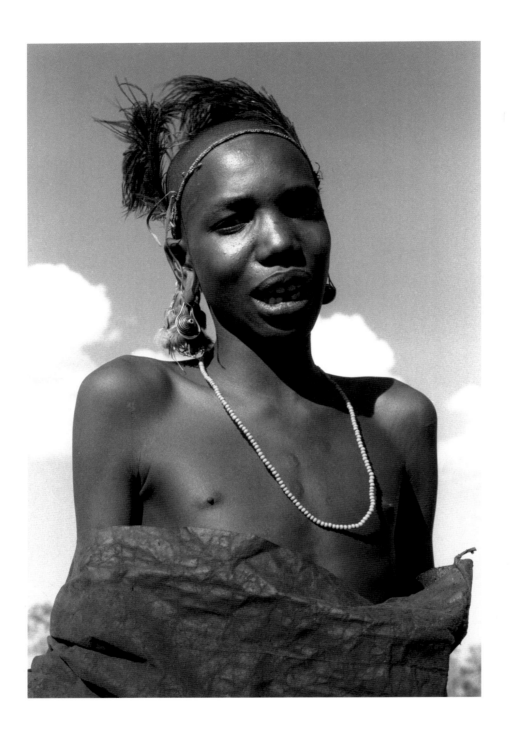

ABOVE Laputa Lekakwar, one of the author's Samburu companions, after circumcision, 1977.

OPPOSITE A young Samburu.

Circumcised Samburu boy with shot birds.

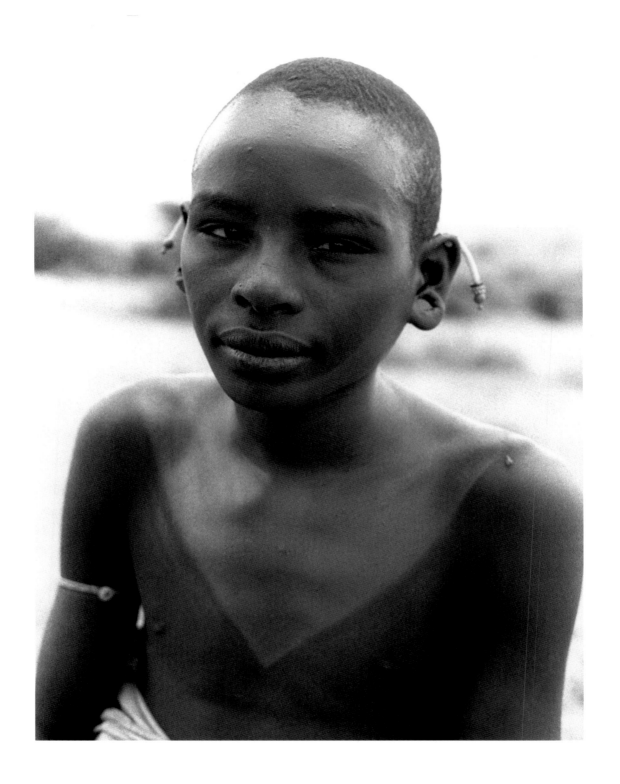

A Samburu initiate.